IN SMALL MEASURE

Language most shows a man:
Speak, that I may see thee.

Ben Jonson, *Discoveries*

In Small Measure

by Christopher Whitby

OPEN POETRY LTD

First published in Great Britain 2011 by
Open Poetry Ltd
Island House
Arthur Street
Barwell
Leicestershire LE9 8AH

info@openpoetry.org.uk
www.openpoetry.org.uk

ISBN: 978-0-9559162-1-2

A CIP record for this title is available from the British Library.

The right of Christopher Whitby to be identified as the author
of this work has been asserted in accordance with the Copyright,
Designs and Patents Act, 1988. © Christopher Whitby 2011

Christopher Whitby's website: chriswhitby.org.uk

Designed by Dragonfly Presentation Graphics Ltd
www.dragonflypg.co.uk

Printed and bound in the UK by the MPG Books Group,
Bodmin and King's Lynn.

CONTENTS

Preface	Page	ix
Acquiring permission to use		xi
Check-up		1
Sleeping Child		2
Slightly Foxed		3
'She Was Rushed into Hospital Last Night'		4
After the Play		5
For a Child's Christening		6
A Refusal to Mourn the Death of a Child		7
Cinders		8
Bookmark		9
Model Railway		10
Waking Child		11
Old Flame		12
Lost Inheritance		13
Flight Plan		14
Balm in Gilead		16
Divining Water		17
Reflections at Buttermere		18
Daddy		19
Violation		20
Reading the Leaves 1916		21
Well Now		22
Just So		23
Making Out		24
Party Frock		25
Breaking Silence		26
Snap		27
The Best Poems		28
Lost Presents		29
Growing Up		30
Through a Glass Darkly		31

Salad Days   34
Interrogation   35
Rex Quondam   36
Like Father, Like Son   37
A Picture Seen When Browsing in a Bookshop   38
For a Colleague   39
The What Ifs   40
Housemove   42
Scafell Pike   43
Neighbour   44
WW1 War Grave, Equancourt   45
Night Exercise   46
Lunacy   47
Rapunzel   48
The Long View   49
Technical Rehearsal   50
Touchdown   51
'Since there's no help' – Drayton   52
Bar Talk   53
The Voice of God Walking in the Garden
                          with a Friend   54
A Promise Made   56
Osric's Tale   57
En Passant   58

Acknowledgements   59
Notes   60

PREFACE

Many of the poems in this volume are intended for oral delivery as much as for reading (an issue which sometimes causes controversy). The poems that are essentially little character monologues, presenting a persona's situation or problem as well as attitude, can be acted as miniscule dramas, either directly towards an audience or towards a mute fellow actor. Many of them have already been acted on stage in an entertainment that intermingles the short character pieces with music (violin, guitar and soprano voice to date), reviving poetry's age-old affinity with music without turning the poetry into song lyric – a connection that in modern times we seem to have all but lost.

The poems do not have to be acted, but it is one expression they lean towards, and it would give me great pleasure to think that they sometimes lived in this way, whether on stage or simply as an individual's 'party piece' (see page xi for information on permissions). At the very least I hope that they are voices in the head.

They are for the most part short. Many are formal, being sonnets, but (I hope) testing the wonderful variety and elasticity of the sonnet that can, to my mind, present 'infinite riches in a little room'. The contemporary sonnet is alive and well, as any glance through a major modern poet's work will testify, and one of the delights of any set of rules (if rules there are, as opposed to just custom and fashion) is to be found in bending and occasionally breaking them, so playing with expectations.

. Some of the poems are what I call 'sentiments' – just a few lines that seek to express with even greater brevity an emotion or situation with a hinted background story. They are not formal structures like the haiku, but distilled thoughts or responses.

The poems are short also because I would like to think that they can be read anywhere: on a short bus or tube journey, in a school break, between the milk and the eggs in a supermarket, in the brief 'if only I had time to read something' minutes between getting into bed after midnight yet again, despite one's best efforts, and turning out the light. Two minutes will cater for a sonnet; a few seconds for a sentiment. I have no dislike of long poems (unless they are dull), but as life seems to pattern itself into ever smaller fragments both for writing and reading, I have moved inexorably towards the short. Besides, you can work on a sonnet in your head while doing other things, although I sometimes wonder whether mentally composing sonnets while behind the wheel of a car may one day become a traffic offence.

Poetry, Verbal Delivery and Acting

Some people loathe hearing actors speak verse, arguing that there is too much expression and emphasis given to certain words and that the subtlety of poetry gets mangled. For my part, I loathe hearing poets (or anyone) speak verse in absolute or near monotones, supposedly 'letting the words do the work by themselves' but to my ear and mind too often presenting the lines as if they were just items on a shopping list.

The nub of the matter is the relationship of poetry to drama. In a review of a television programme on John Donne, the critic A. A. Gill neatly summed up one side of the debate by writing that 'poetry isn't drama: the imposition of character, the inflection of emotion and opinion, diminishes it. Nobody will ever read you Donne or Shakespeare's sonnets or Eliot with more poignancy and meaning, more beautifully, than the voice in your head' (*Culture, The Sunday Times*, 31 May 2009).

In many ways I agree, but I have to reply that very frequently plays are also more poignant and meaningful in the head. Nearly *all* writing is: poetry has no special rights here. I've seen some very good productions of *King*

Lear as well as some mediocre ones, but nothing betters my imagined Lear (though constantly informed of course by the performances I watch). This is partly because when we read, ambiguities of tone and of character do not need to be resolved in the mind and we can keep contradictions and variations in suspension; on stage, however, a decision needs to be made about 'how to play it'. A prime example is Macbeth's reaction to the news of his wife's death: 'She should have died hereafter.' In reading it silently, I can keep all the shades between rampant rage and dulled sterility up in the air, not because I have some neutral tone in my mind's ear, but because I can imagine all the possible dramatic tones simultaneously. Neutral mechanistic delivery does not keep these options open; it simply speaks of mechanistic neutrality. Absence of expression orally is an expression.

But that's why I still go to the theatre and see new productions of plays I already know well. That's the glory of it: the text is the seed from which my imagination and a theatre company can grow and harvest new ideas and responses. Each production is a new rendition.

I believe the same is true of poetry. Some poems lend themselves more to a spoken or acted realisation than others, and many of mine are written with the voice in mind. To say that poetry should not be given to actors, however, is to conceive that there is somehow a near-definitive silent version, that 'the voice in your head' has little to learn from anyone else's rendition and that a poem cannot or should not be realised differently over and over and over again. Like a play. The problem is not acting, but bad acting: stealing the show. Perhaps because actors are used to inhabiting characters, they may sometimes over-invent when there is barely any character to be.

And before it was placed on an esoteric pedestal, poetry – even short non-narrative poetry – was an oral tradition, reinterpreted with each delivery. I'd like to put some of that potential back into circulation.

I trust both readers and actors will find something worthwhile, not least some characters, in this collection. And to be frank, even an overblown rendition is arguably a better fate for a fair poem (if it is) than silence.

To Note or Not

When selections of the poems have been acted, the event programmes have always contained some brief notes concerning references that might not be within the immediate reach or experience of all the audience. They are, after all, not in a good position to look up any of these during the performance. Theatre programmes frequently carry plot summaries and explanatory notes to help the audience through a play experienced perhaps for the first time.

It seems a courtesy to provide some similar notes in this book (placed at the back). For a start it makes the book more portable. I would like to save readers from the need to google if I can – it sounds like a noble endeavour – or I would like at the very least to offer for efficiency's sake a little direction on what might be searched for, if a reader should wish to follow up any reference that seems worth pursuing. There is of course no obligation to look at them, but if you do, I hope they are of interest. If you are doubtful, think of them as just part of the programme supplied for the theatre in the head. *Beginners' call.*

Christopher Whitby

ACQUIRING PERMISSION TO USE

All three of the sonnets that are contained under the title 'Through a Glass Darkly' (pages 31-33) can be performed, broadcast or printed by anyone without breach of copyright providing three simple conditions are observed:

1. There is no alteration to the words
2. The poems are not used in connection with any illegal, pornographic or otherwise exploitative material or context
3. Christopher Whitby's authorship is acknowledged in the chosen media

As for performing or using any of the other poems in this volume in a public situation, please contact the publisher (Open Poetry Ltd) either by post or email, using the details below. In most instances, confirmation of having purchased the book will be sufficient for an individual performer in a one-off event and easy terms can be reached for amateur groups.

Permission *must* be obtained before any poems are printed, or are broadcast via any electronic media, including the internet. In most cases permission will easily be granted, but failure to request and obtain it in advance of publication will be deemed a breach of copyright.

Open Poetry Ltd
Island House
Arthur Street
Barwell
Leicestershire LE9 8AH

info@openpoetry.org.uk

Check-up

I am OK. No, really, life's a blast,
if that's what you still say these days. It's true
I do forget some things. The distant past
is clear as I could wish. It's just what's new,
what happened yesterday, last week, that's where
I come adrift, but is that any more
than simple ageing, all the wear and tear
of burning candles at both ends? I'm sure
it's nothing. Though there is... one tiny doubt.
You see, it's when I wake I don't recall,
some days, my leaving such a mess, clothes out,
the window open, marks along the wall.
And in my mouth a little blood. All fine,
but here's the thing. It doesn't taste like mine.

Sleeping Child

As I carry you
cradled in my arms,
I picture refugees
and feel the dead weight of you
against my heart.

Slightly Foxed

Sigs B5r to C4v have not been
cut, which makes me wonder quite what I should
do. What would the library say if I were seen
to take a knife– consider also what would
be their view if that same knife should then turn out
to be not sharp enough and the pages torc
even just a teensy bit. Would someone shout
at me in all this rustling quietness, or
simply fix me with a stare, then lean down for
a word? 'Your ticket, Sir, if you don't mind,
and now let me escort you to the door.
You seem unmindful of the rules you signed.'
Of course, I'll end up doing what is right,
no matter what adventure seems in sight.

'She Was Rushed into Hospital Last Night'

It's one of those sharp,
optimistic
spring mornings,
but only fear
is rising
to light the day.

After the Play
(Peter Quince Remembers)

Unforgettable – our fifteen minutes
of fame. Although I would not want to see
those days come back – not them. It was as if
the rhythm of our lives had somehow
skipped a beat and we were made to dance
to someone else's tune. You don't believe?
That's your bad luck. Unsettling things they are,
that mar more than they mend, God save us all.

We were not called again, but then so what?
We just went back to what we did before –
that's life. It might have changed, but it did not.
It's what it is and only fools want more.
The magic died afore we realised,
and yet – for one brief moment – we were *prized*.

For a Child's Christening
(at which it was sung)

If all the world's a stage, then be the fool
and speak your mind, without offence, to all,
whatever parts they play. And in the school
of wit find wisdom and the verve to call
to strict account whatever seems to bear
no sense, or right, or goodness in its heart.
Life has its luck. The trick is not to care
how much or little Fortune holds your part,
but taking all with equal thanks and grace,
in looking sideways at the world's affairs,
reveal the truths that lie behind the face
and light the dark that coats us unawares.
So, motley minded and obliquely just,
be yet a touchstone in whom all may trust.

A Refusal to Mourn the Death of a Child

If I were
to choose a memory,
it would be
when lion and tiger
first came to tea.

They're shut away now,
like everything else.

Cinders

To tell the truth, I tried quite hard to kick
the other one off, as I bolted free
to save my shame. I made it in the nick
of time, but, oh, my feet were killing me!
Glass slippers... for a ball! Who dreamed up that?
A long walk back as well, always in doubt
I'd beat the sisters home. Yet there I sat,
as if nothing had happened while they'd been out.
And then at last he came. You know the rest.
Except you don't. I have exchanged one cage
for another. Bigger, yes, but now I wage
small wars with courtiers over each request
and bound by protocol against my will,
I weep to find myself in service still.

Bookmark

After the funeral my brother said,
'I'll sort the books.' I wondered why. Suppose
our mother wanted them untouched – all those
raw memories bound up in what he'd read.
So later I was quite relieved to see
most shelves still full. The boxes in the hall
contained 'his other wives': the sea in all
its moods and sailing ships. No use to me,
and yet I took back what I'd given. Then
tucked inside an Alexander Kent I saw
the bookmark. Was this at his bedside when
he at last conceded he would read no more?
They float now by my bed, but I've not dared
to read his last words among so many shared.

Model Railway

With figures on the stations all to scale,
the trains run dead on time.
A jolt runs through the rolling stock:
the cattle trucks in line.

Waking Child

When you wake
you often cry,
and as I cuddle you,
I wonder:
is it loss or relief
that so stabs your heart?

Old Flame

For God's sake, Peter, look at me. Do I
still own the face you loved? I'm forty-two,
with children of my own. I don't know why
you've come... Oh no, oh not for *them*. If you
so much as dream of that, you can fu– fly
off back to Neverland for good. Make do
with what you've got – eternal youth. Just try
to come to terms with it. Just think it through.

I'm sorry, I'm not meaning to be rude
but face it, we were always worlds apart.
There is no meeting point. You just delude
yourself to think I'd keep you in my heart.
If all our thoughts were wishes, we'd still not make them
                                                rhyme.
Not growing up's your penance. Doing so is mine.

Lost Inheritance

"You can tell whose son you are," my mum would say,
especially when I'd irritated her
by being me, but with each faltering day
I know my father less. When we inter
the bones, we bury the memories too –
not that he ever spoke much of his life
or I ever asked. The bare facts I knew
but not his doubts or any inner strife
he might have struggled to contain throughout the years.
If we could somehow have our time again
I'd force him to confess his deepest fears
and what he'd seen and done that caused most pain.
I am his son, and give his goodness due,
but need to feel his heart of darkness too.

Flight Plan

It wasn't the sun that burned my wings
but the idea.

To transcend my element, you think?
No. No, it was much simpler than that –
to leave behind the grime, the unremitting work,
the sheer boredom of it all,
and that unbending man, so hard to love,
whose head was so full of ideas, he had
no space for anyone else,
and who would have sacrificed the whole world
to prove one principle of design.

And yet, I have to say, the flying was
astonishing. He had that right.
The updraft glide, the sideslip turn,
the breath-defying swoop,
so many impulses of delight
as if one might reach out and touch

whatever.

To look down and see the world laid bare
as you could hardly then imagine:
the tiny, tiny people at work, at play,
at war, the hills unravelling to knit themselves
again and, drifting down, the mapped out details:
a theatre of furrows, a ram in a thicket,
a knife laid by,

but all just rotting in the dirt.

No, I did not circle higher
to touch the sun,
but to send the earth
further
and further
away.

Balm in Gilead

Her faith,
the rector said,
stood fast
until the end.

But I know
that she died
of complications.

Divining Water

I tried it once at school, this savage art,
with country friends and twigs untimely ripped
from hedges by the road. Tight fisted and tight lipped
they swore they were real hazel, and we stripped
the bark from some for scientific test
of which configuration worked the best –
no thought that we might fail. In line abreast
close by a gurgling drain we made our start.
Yet only I was made to feel the wood spring back
and buck against the pressure of my grip.
I laughed and said it was a joke, a slip,
and tried to hold it nonchalantly slack.
I mock it still, but with each year that comes
I learn to dread the pricking of my thumbs.

Reflections at Buttermere

This is the lake of glass,
through which I see
new mountains undisturbed
resting their heads on a flecked blue veld.

A shell of alter egos,
where seagulls landing on the thin divide
must paddle toe to toe with doubtful friends
and sharp-beaked terns stab rivals in the face.

Along the shore
a heron stands
with one foot rooted in another world
and balefully hunched refuses to look down.

"It's beautiful,"
you say, forgetting that I've seen
the charming mirror crack from side to side
and let a second self come stepping through.

I throw a stone,
upsetting you,
but saving us and any passing god
the horror of meeting ourselves complete.

Daddy

When I was two
my father carried me outside
and showed me the moon, bright and full.
I fell in love, and miss him still.

Violation

I am all the daughters of my father's house,
And all the brothers too: and yet I know not.

Twelfth Night, II, iv

What don't I know? Not just if Seb still lives –
though how we need a body, warm or cold.
It's what I have and may become that gives
me sleepless nights. Shall I grow old
in this disguise, androgenized by time,
an exile from my sex as well as home?
Or will some carpe diem act mean I'm
condemned to states yet further from my own?
He favours me. They whisper that's not chance,
but in what way? Is he *too much* the man?
Her beauty's stunning. Dodging her advance
is hard. Why not take what and where I can?
I'm shipwrecked twice, more helpless than before,
Afraid to drown, afraid to reach the shore.

Reading the Leaves 1916

The next few hours remain a mystery,
but if you had the time for just one book,
what would it be? A fiction I assume.
Under the circumstances history
appears quite futile and religion plies
a dying trade. Yet could you bear to look
inside some novels now? We may presume
henceforth the comedy of manners lies
in no man's land. A play? But we have Lears
aplenty. So when all comes down to chance
is poetry what's left to mask our fears?
How many Palgraves deck the mud of France?
The whistles blow. Good luck. Wish me the same,
and if we meet again... I'll ask your name.

Well Now

My mother sometimes used to say
how much she still
missed her father,
a man I scarcely knew.

Now as she braves widowhood,
I too drop a stone
and do not hear a splash.

Just So

The camel just said... 'Humph!' Elizabeth
replies – she does a good 'Humph!' – but as I
watch her smile, something snatches at my breath
and I am adrift on a Medusa raft
of memories, eyeing each other up.
I feel the water lap about my thigh
as my father sitting by my bath reads 'Humph!'
and grins a scowl with all his storyteller's craft.

A younger son, I don't expect to feel
the weight of family continuity or
have tradition dragging at my heel,
and yet... and yet, I'd almost ask for more
if he and I could co-exist again
and fuse, O Best Beloved, my now and then.

Making Out

Sometimes I think I got it all wrong. Not
just a turning missed, a fork to the right
instead of left, but a start all to pot,
back to front, upside down, inside out, quite
hopelessly muddled, off on the wrong foot,
stumbling head over heels, arse about face,
all fingers and thumbs, both feet somehow put
down the same trouser leg, an utter disgrace.
But then the point of balance need not lie
dead centre for a movement to run true
and goals are just an attitude of mind.
So in eccentric travel I may try
the better part of what there is to do
and more than those who never look behind.

Party Frock

'Give us a twirl,' I said and so she did
(thus marking out some territory – men
don't do twirls). Weaving straps and flounce she hid
herself behind the conjured image, then
with new-spun adult confidence enquired:
'You think?' 'You'll slay them all,' I said, not sure
if that was quite the answer she required
but sensing needs not prominent before.

Oh take it off! Put on your jeans again.
Let me be Mr Grumpkin still. In such
small acts I feel you slipping through the cup
my hands once made for you and hate it when
you bring me face to face with just how much
I want-admire-resent your growing up.

Breaking Silence

There was a time you'd climb a mountain top
and find yourself alone to contemplate
whatever promptings God, your inner soul,
or nature's trenchant silence might evoke.
To do that now, you have to beat the dawn
or settle for arrival with the dusk,
having doggedly threaded through the Goretex exodus
to curious looks and snippets of sharp advice.
Now mountains keep their counsel through the day,
but met at the right hour will whisper still
the old familiar charm: "All this I give
to you, as far as eye can see, and more,
if you will but bow down and worship me."
Enveloped in the mist, I bend my knee.

Snap

With toast and one too many cups of coffee
I scan the parents' grief. The usual stuff:
'an angel with a smile for everyone';

'A lovely personality', 'a joy',
'a friend'; 'her whole life stood before her, now
cut short by mindless violence'.

Back home from ballet class, Louise demands
a piggy-back across the crocodiles
that lie, I know, all down our hall.

Three steps across their snouts, and wary of
the twitching tails, I sense a subtle shift
of weight and cannot stop a surge

of boundless terror at what lies ahead.

I snatch at common sense, but in my mind
a stain soaks quietly, as did the ring
that lurks beneath our pretty sideboard vase.

The Best Poems

The best poems are not creative
but archaeology. You dust away
life's debris from something nagging you it's there.
I think this is a hand. But as you scrape,
you find it is a foot, though not where you
expected. *Should I move it where I think
it ought to be? Or leave it, a testament
to how this body's lain these thousand years?*

A shaper of words. A remover of silt,
more like. Dig too hard and you churn away
dry roots and dormant seeds to find your gold.
Take a soft brush, and you will write
what, in a sense, has always been written,
but never seen entire before.

Lost Presents

Without wanting to, I knew what they were
the moment I saw the coloured wrap.
We were doing so well,
all things considered. Now this.

Whoever they were from, and I did
not want to know, were missing
thank yous, now beyond repair –
but I have learned to be uncurious.

Damn it, we thought we were doing so well,
all things... well, not all things, it seems.
I cried a bit of course (how could I not?)
but these things are and will not change,

so I found a bag and put them in the car
for dropping at the tip next time I passed.
Another secret burial
like so many gone before.

Growing Up

When I fell,
Daddy would catch me,
always. Then one day
he wasn't there
and I fell all the way.

Through a Glass Darkly
A Christmas triptych – three voices in search of reason

1. The Fourth Magus

Another star? And why should that mean more
than the last, recorded in the books
we all have read? Our peoples being sore
afraid, did the world mend its ways or looks,
or (may he rest in peace) to borrow my
old tutor's hat, what evidence was there
that men improved, grew good, that God on high
brought peace on earth or changed things anywhere?

You'll go? In curiosity or trust?
No matter, you will see what you will see
and reach your own conclusions as you must.
The wonder will be if you all agree.
Yet bring me word. If you do not, well, so;
for if God's kingdom comes, *shall we not know?*

2. Joseph

Caught between God and Caesar, that's me,
Not to mention Herod, and our Liz
who's also had a boy, as like to his
father... as any little angel ought to be.
I know what people think. But it's a fact
that Liz is past the age, and who would swear
that Mary lies? Still, it's safer here where
only sheep and oxen talk behind our back.

The son I've always wanted, eh? May be.
But will he carry on the trade and take
good care of us when we are old and make
us proud and be our boy? These strange guests see
something else. Well, in time he'll find his voice,
but if this is God's child, we have no choice.

3. The Shepherd

Find my sheep, he said, find my lost lambs. Well now,
I says to him, that's easier said than done.
You know how many wolves there are? And how
they'll lie in wait for hours for just one
kill? Forgive them too, he says, they know
not what they do. Oh yes they bloody do, I say,
or him as made them does. Forgive? You show
us how. He stopped, quite still, and then just turned away.

Now when he was a babe, the magic rolled
all over us. We heard the angels sing.
We thought the time had come, you know, as told –
God's peace, wrongs righted, all that sort of thing.
It didn't happen. Something did. But planned?
Well you tell me. I still don't understand.

Salad Days

I haven't written a poem for you
for forty years. I feel a bitter shame
at that, since it was largely due
to your departure that I ever wrote at all,
Well, that and holding God to blame.
I had a fire then, when death was new
and righteous indignation fanned the flame
of such creative gifts as I might call
my own. And then, half unremarked, a day
arrived when I could write without my fix of pain.
O brave new world ! Yet it's banal to say
my writing could be anything but vain,
For looking back, one thing I plainly see:
I never wrote for you. I wrote for me.

Interrogation

It would be better if you told us what
we want to know now. You've been in this game
for long enough to know you're dead. It's not
the when but how that is at stake. A shame,
of course, in other times.... but let that go.
What can I say to make your case more plain?
Our people are... creative, skilled. They know
about the careful management of pain.

You wonder what I am and why I choose
this work – a man with family, like you.
They think I'm in accounts, which is quite true
if you– Excuse me. Yes? Ah, good. Good news!
You are reprieved. Though not released, not yet.
We have your child. Let's watch her pay your debt.

Rex Quondam

So now at last the final battle waits.
I have no hope that Merlin will appear.
                    O sing me the songs of Avalon
I doubt there's magic strong enough in all
the world to change the course of these events
which will consume us all. We yield our days
                    and lay me down like a child
not to the dark of some triumphant evil
but to the greyness that is history.
Our kindling light will just be once upon a time.
My own flesh rebels and I am weary–
                    I have no wanting for the dawn
I could not start again, not even for
the grail, which, truth to tell, I know devoured
our fellowship. What's left I should desire now?
                    since death my heart beguiled
Out with the candles. Let but one remain
To light us to our graves and show our dreams were vain.

Like Father, Like Son

Visiting my mother
last night, dog tired,
I fell asleep in my father's chair.

I wonder if she thought
he had come back
from the dead.

A Picture Seen When Browsing in a Bookshop

They stand in line, their shaven heads
an affront. Loose limbed, but ill at ease,
a few glance at the camera. The rest
watch mutely as an officer strides by
with purpose in his boots. The trees behind
stand guard in mocking stripes of light and dark
beside a building housing God knows what,
for these, the caption tells, are woods near Buchenwald.

A lifetime on, the focus is the man
unseen behind the lens. What was this for?
Admin? A souvenir? Or did he plan
to show the kids this part of Daddy's war?
And this disturbing thought keeps edging through –
that I'm compelled to share his point of view.

For a Colleague

We had our golden age, though we did not
know it at the time, when laughter ran
down the corridors between our lives,
and we lived off the youth of those we taught.
Now Patti's gone, and Butty, and do you recall
"But my dear you can't buy a sleeve for that!"
Such flamboyance, such a bitter end,
Yet few, I think, so bitter as Patti's.
We marvel at how well you do – as one does –
but do not know the half. It suits us well
to keep this piece of ignorance intact
lest we fall prey to fears too deep to think.
You stand guard for us, our veteran,
shouldering experience we do not want to own.

The What Ifs

It's the three in the morning sweats
and the what ifs are crowding round the bed.
Tonight I sense them ganging up
to form the shadow of our child.

Whatever I believe by day,
in these dark corners I have learned
I could without a hesitation kill
if someone if so much as if

but as she fades I know I do not know
if strength I claim is Brighton rocked in me.

I've felt the sabre slash of childhood death
but only as a child, to hold all in
until excused the meal to march
up to my room and curse all living things,

but I can't hold my breath so long these days
and I am wrapped in thinner skin than then.
So what if now if now, they say,
if she should if so much as if,

what will you be if if becomes not if?
If not of her, then what remains of you?

This is not popping out, another room,
as if back soon to have a cup of tea.
Donne knew the score, at midnight's stroke
of dear dead Lucy's nothing re-begot.

And Christ just piled the guilt on loss – one death
for all, so weep no more. The ancients knew:
Prometheus' liver grew again each night,
and Sisyphus – within an inch each day.

The what if early hours will pass
and yet I shall and shall not sleep again.

Housemove

Cathy is hardly out the door before Jane is moving in.
Such is the way of things. It's all agreed –
no fuss, no scenes, and by consent of all,
no strings, especially of the kind that pull
when least expected or desired.
But as Jane settles in and sorts things out,
she cannot help but note the light dust rings
where Cathy's ornaments once stood and doubt
a lingering warmth within the chair
that she most favoured.
As her new Adam smiles towards a bed
slumped in strange contours (and a hint of scent?),
she knows her eager choice was not his first
and feels the tug of her she has displaced.

Scafell Pike

Half way, we questioned whether to go on
and then again, ten minutes from the top,
Much less in doubt than to reaffirm the need
within was stronger than the hurtling sleet
that sliced our cheeks, froze lips and closed our eyes.
Bent double, old beggars under sacks indeed,
we pivoted our coming and our going
on outstretched fingers brushing ice-rimed cairn.
When steaming gently in the heated car
we asked once more why on earth we did this,
we knew our answers would not be the same.
For me, remembering turning back from other goals,
I know no better spur to my intent
than because I am here.

Neighbour

This is the
first time
I've worn a suit for her.

With respect,
my hands drift past
the black tie.

WW1 War Grave, Equancourt

The stones seem to ruffle in the breeze
but no vision comes. I really cannot grasp
the enormity of what happened here.
The fragments of old film, the books,
even the poetry do not prepare
the heart or mind for standing here,
as if in trespass, with no cataclysm
of my own to measure out this loss, this waste.
It looks 'complete', from two VCs to died of wounds
two weeks after armistice, just turned eighteen.
And yet there's more. In the visitors' book
from nineteen ninety-five an entry reads:
'Dad, my children have helped me to find you
at last.'

Night Exercise

The night the soldiers came for him they had
their guns of course, but one bright soul had thought
to bring a spade, for if their man became
a frigging pain, they might perhaps be glad
of it when all the fun was gone. They caught
him in his bed, quite unaware his name
had been passed on by someone he'd once met.

There was, tonight, no time to rape his wife,
so where the wood curls round the valley's head
the questioning was rifle-butt hard. 'Now
dig,' they said at last, but with no hope of life,
he would not help them. So they shot him dead,
and dug, and covered him, and trod him down,
and hated him, because he'd made them sweat.

Lunacy

Among the frogs that friggle in our pond
there may well be a prince or two entranced
in a career break, and on the lake beyond,
perhaps a princess flapped her wings, then danced
again last night before she slipped away,
serene above and furious underneath.
And who can tell that for the length of one bright day
a whole new village won't adorn the heath.
Why not? For if imagination wills,
the mountains ought to move, and tales like these
beat in the blood. The reasoning that kills
our fears may hide the woods among the trees.
I only know that, as the sun sinks down,
I hear the wolves howl at the edge of town.

Rapunzel

It was well known
that one flick of her head
could send a would-be suitor
flying fifty yards.

The night I tried my luck
the window ledge was almost in my grasp
when with a sudden flash of blades
she gave herself a bob.

The Long View

Galileo Galilei,
by the living God that made me,
thinks the stars are to be read just like a book.
He's discovered something odd
in the handiwork of God
and has offered me his telescope to look.

I've turned the offer down
on the fundamental ground
that he's putting faith where faith ought not to be.
However much it grieves us,
our eyes may still deceive us
and truth is rarely found in what we see.

I don't think he's a bad man,
but he's acting like a madman
and he'll find himself in trouble soon, no doubt.
To tip the world up on its arse
for what appears through bits of glass
is a folly we can all well do without.

Technical Rehearsal

He's dying. As he calls me to the mark
I know he's dying – and I know he won't
give up. They never do, these lighting crew.
They're always last to leave and yet they don't
need drama, passion in the way we do,
we shadows of the stage that fear the dark.
Effect, and change, effect. Creation's fuse
rekindled, shaped and put once more to use.

Don't know his last name. Doubt I ever will.
So here lies... John, who lit his last scene on –
who knows? Effect, and change, effect, until
the final cue, then pack the gear and gone
to light some other stage. Well here's to you,
to the last can and shutter, here's to you.

Touchdown

When I was young, unknown,
I wanted to be famous.
Now, flying in to share a private grief,
I am afraid the fruits of my success
will prove too tart for comfort or compassion.
Homespun George is dead.
Carol soldiers on – of course she would –
but Amy, newly pregnant, must wonder at the trick
that makes fathers so quick to leave her.
I fiddle with the strap, but know the fear
is of an image cheaply strewn
across five million breakfasts.

I long to pass through customs unremarked,
but as I touch the earth and rumble to a halt,
I hear the cameras click.

'Since there's no help'
by Michael Drayton (1563-1632)

Since there's no help, come let us kiss and part;
Nay, I have done, you get no more of me,
And I am glad, yea glad with all my heart
That thus so cleanly I myself can free;
Shake hands forever, cancel all our vows,
And when we meet at any time again,
Be it not seen in either of our brows
That we one jot of former love retain.
Now at the last gasp of Love's latest breath,
When, his pulse failing, Passion speechless lies,
When Faith is kneeling by his bed of death,
And Innocence is closing up his eyes,
Now if thou wouldst, when all have given him over,
From death to life thou mightst him yet recover.

Guest spot. Why? – see notes on page 65.

Bar Talk

The world is full of widows. You know that?
Here, take this wedding photograph for one
example. That one's gone, and him, the fat
one at the back, and them two, but the sun
still shines on all their wives. Does that seem fair?
I tell you man to man that we've been passed
the bunch of shorter straws when you compare –
as women say, men don't know how to last.

And him – my son – he's good as dead, you'd say.
Poor mutt left both his legs and half his brain
beside an Afghan road. I'm on my way
to visit, but there's no-one home 'cept pain,
nor will be... Sink one more? Hey, make it two,
but then I'm out. There's... something I must do.

The Voice of God Walking in the Garden, with a Friend

Of course, foreknowledge is a tricky thing
when free will's also in your gift.
I found it helped to give them just one rule;
there'd be no question which they broke
and in a universe where time has been
made infinite, eventually they would.

You ask if it has made me happier.
Hard judgement for a God that knows too much.
It makes *them* happier... at times,
on balance... now and then?
When all the sums are done.

And at its heart was language, yes,
though not that old Adamic stuff the scholars love,
all words and things that are the same,
but this – with that first bite
was born the true comparative
and with the next, superlative,
to hang upon and qualify the Word.

And worth the pain? Oh certainly for me,
for until then it was all rather bland and see
the roles I then could play as things went on.
There was a time when people wrote them down.
For them? Well let's just say
it keeps them on their toes.

And what would you have wanted me to do?
Just loaf around all day and be?
And more than that, exist unneeded?
I might as well just vanish up
my own ineffability.

No, no, take my advice. One simple rule
is all it needs. And when all things are possible,
the odds they disobey become quite probable
and in one version of events inevitable. Grasp that
and let the other outcomes slip away
(remember that in some you don't exist).

If omnia unum est, it just boils down to this:
for all the loss, you win and so do they.
And God – my little joke – it's fun,
believe me, do.

A Promise Made

When she was ten,
she blithely said
that if she died
and I still lived,
she'd haunt me
in my dreams.

She does,
she does.

Osric's Tale

He called me a waterfly. I heard him
plain as I'm standing here. Said it to his friend –
good looking boy, and cultured in a way
you don't often find round here – but not for me,
not... not with... *you know*. Oh, call it a whim
if you like – the hat – but for him to send
me up like that! I was in the king's pay,
a right royal messenger. So was he
really mad, you ask. I think not. Sharp, sly,
cruel, bitter, twisted even, but he knew
what he was doing, oh yes, so why should I
be sorry that he's dead? I'll tell you why.
Now we must learn Norwegian ways, who's who,
what's in, what's out, what words can make you die.

En Passant

I've walked from Porlock,
thought I'd just drop by.
The news? Oh nothing much,
nothing of
importance.
You?

ACKNOWLEDGEMENTS

Some of these poems have previously appeared in *Orogenic Zones* comp. Terry Gifford and Rosie Smith, *Blood Line* (Blinking Eye Publishing), *The Chimaera*, *14 by 14*, *Lucid Rhythms*, Kaleidoscope (BBC Radio 4).

'Check-Up' was a finalist for the 2009 Nemerov Award.

NOTES

It is very difficult to gauge the currency of what once was or at least seemed to be a shared heritage, but that is true for every generation. We do not learn all the same things that our parents did and they lose touch with our common experience, as we do with our children. These notes are not intended to insult anyone's intelligence, but just to assist as different generations and cultures may find useful.

There are a number of variations, even experiments with metre in the sonnets. This is not the place for any discourse on that, but there are some observations at www.chriswhitby.org.uk/ism-metre

Slightly Foxed – The title is a pun on booktraders' descriptions of some old books as 'slightly foxed', meaning there are a few brown spots on the pages (a result of age), and of course the meaning of foxed as perplexed. 'Sigs' is a bibliophile's common abbreviation for 'signatures' – in old books, large printed sheets were folded down to the book size before binding and each folded set often marked with a 'signature' (e.g. A, B, C) on the first page made, rather than page numbers being used. Individual pages can be referred to by their signature and leaf number from the start of that folded set, using recto ('r' for short) and verso ('v') to identify whether a right hand or left hand (reverse) page. Thus a modern page 5 might be Sig. A3r. Often the book buyer was responsible for cutting the sheets at the outer edge folds and in some old books this has not been done.

After the Play – Peter Quince, a carpenter, was the director of the play *Pyramus and Thisbe* performed by the Mechanicals (working men) in front of Duke Theseus and his 'set' in Shakespeare's *A Midsummer Night's Dream*. The actors were chased around, or led a merry dance by Puck during their rehearsal in the forest. Having performed their play before the Duke, they might perhaps have thought that their futures could be about to change.

For a Child's Christening – This was set for four voices (SATB) by Eleanor Graff-Baker (www.efgraff-baker.co.uk). There are a number of Shakespearean references, especially to *As You Like It* in which the (far from stupid) Fool is Touchstone.

A Refusal to Mourn the Death of a Child – The title is a part borrowing from the title of the poem by Dylan Thomas, *A Refusal to Mourn the Death, by Fire, of A Child in London,* but interpreted differently – no reasoned argument, just a closing down. Knowledge of the Thomas poem, especially its tone, does act as a particular foil for this shorter piece.

Bookmark – Alexander Kent is a pseudonym of Douglas Reeman when writing novels about life in the Royal Navy during the Napoleonic wars.

Old Flame – Wendy and Peter Pan, or just a mature woman and a former lover who won't 'grow up', as some men don't in women's eyes? Performance in this instance does not demand that a choice be made.

Lost Inheritance – 'Heart of darkness' is borrowed from the title of Joseph Conrad's novel with a few of its echoes.

Flight Plan – The 'unbending man' is Daedalus (whose name in Greek means 'cunning worker'), father of Icarus. The end of the third stanza echoes 'a lonely impulse of delight' in W. B. Yeats' poem *An Irish Airman Forsees His Death* and 'as if one might reach out and touch' makes a knowing glance at *High Flight* by spitfire pilot John Gilllespie Magee Jr:

> Up, up the long, delirious burning blue
> I've topped the wind-swept heights with easy grace
> Where never lark, or ever eagle flew –
> And, while with silent, lifting mind I've trod
> The high untrespassed sanctity of space,
> Put out my hand, and touched the face of God.

In Breughel's painting *Fall of Icarus* (which now inevitably also conjures up Auden's great poem *Musée des Beaux Arts)*, a ram, knife and 'theatre of furrows' can be seen. The ram in the thicket and the knife also refer to the biblical episode in which Abraham nearly sacrifices his son Isaac on God's command (Genesis ch. 22, vv. 1-24; the King James Bible uses the word 'thicket', which gives an instantly recognisable context if you grew up with KJ, but not if you didn't).

Balm in Gilead – The title is a reference to the Old Testament and to a well-known traditional African-American spiritual, the lyrics of which refer to the New Testament message of salvation through Christ. The Balm of Gilead is interpreted as a spiritual medicine that is able to heal Israel and so sinners in general. In the Old Testament, the balm of Gilead is referred to in Jeremiah Ch. 8 v. 22: 'Is there no balm in Gilead? Is there no physician there? Why then is there no healing for the wounds of my people?'

The spiritual begins:

> There is a balm in Gilead
> To make the wounded whole;
> There is a balm in Gilead
> To heal the sin-sick soul.

Divining Water – It neither aids nor diminishes the poem to say that the main event is true and it is a very strange experience when you are 14. I have not been able to recreate it in adulthood except through the poem. There are several echoes of *Macbeth* – line 2: 'untimely ripped'; line 7: 'If we should fail?'; line 14: 'By the pricking of my thumbs/something wicked this way comes.' The triplet rhyme may or may not add anything but was fun to try.

Reflections at Buttermere – Lake Buttermere in the Lake District is truly a lake of glass, as remarkably frequently its surface remains utterly calm and mirror-like even when other lakes close by are ruffled by wind.

Violation – This does require the reader to be acquainted with the plot of Shakespeare's *Twelfth Night.*

Reading the Leaves 1916 – I trust it soon becomes clear that the setting is the trenches of World War One (when acted I have used a tin hat and a rifle). The title puns on reading books and on reading tea-leaves to tell the future. Line 10: Shakespeare's King Lear, who goes mad and is perhaps the stage's most tragic figure. Line 12: Palgrave's *Golden Treasury* was a popular poetry anthology of the time. Line 13: whistles being blown was the signal to 'go over the top' of the trench, advancing into the enemy fire.

Just So – The key to this is 'How the Camel got his Hump' in the *Just So* stories of Rudyard Kipling, which all children should have read to them. 'O Best Beloved' (line 14) is a phrase used by the narrator to the child listener. The Medusa (Méduse) was the flagship of a small French expedition sent to receive the colony of Senegal from the British. It foundered off the coast in 1816, and while its captain and officers sailed away in well-provisioned lifeboats, 146 men and one woman were herded onto a makeshift raft stocked with a few tubs of wine and some soggy biscuits. Few survived and cannibalism was believed to have occurred. 'The Raft Of The Medusa' is now best known as the painting which sealed the reputation of one of France's greatest painters, Théodore Géricault. It is a strange mixture of the comforting and the unsettling to find yourself reading a story to your child that your own father read to you when you were a child.

Breaking Silence – Line 7: Goretex is a waterproof 'breathable' material used in some of the best mountain jackets and overtrousers. Line 8: generally it is considered unsafe to climb hills or mountains before dawn or arrive at summits so late as to mean the descent will be in the dark, and other walkers will firmly tell you so. Line 11: 'all this' recalls Satan to Jesus on the mountain top (The Temptation, as it is sometime known – Luke ch. 4).

Through a Glass Darkly – The overarching title for these sonnets is taken from one of the most famous passages of St Paul – Corinthians I ch. 13, v. 12: 'For now we see through a glass, darkly; but then face to face: now I know in part; but then shall I know even as also I am known.'

The Fourth Magus – The Bethlehem star was not first new star ever recorded – that was in 1200 BC. Line 3: 'sore afraid' is borrowed from the Bible, Luke ch. 2, v. 9, although there it is applied to the shepherds. Line 13: 'bring me word' recalls Herod's instruction to the Magi: 'Go and search diligently for the young child; and when ye have found him, bring me word again, that I may come and worship him also' (Matthew ch. 2, v. 8).

Joseph – Mary's cousin Elizabeth was also visited by an angel who promised she would give birth – to the boy known later as John the Baptist. The miracle here is that Elizabeth was past child-bearing age.

The Shepherd – There is no reference in the Bible to any of the nativity shepherds meeting Jesus later in his life or watching the final events, but it is not unreasonable to see it as possible within the context. Line 5: 'Forgive them for they know not what they do' are part of Jesus's words from the cross according to Luke (ch. 24, v. 34).

Rex Quondam – King Arthur, *rex quondam et futurus* ('the once and future king'), though in the title the *futurus* is deliberately absent. The Houseman like quatrain in italics has been sung by soprano voice to a haunting melody when performed, but could equally well be whispered, the notion being to have the character saying one thing while the audience is also made privy to other simultaneous thoughts of his. In performance, the last line has been spoken by Arthur as he drives his sword back into a stone.

For a Colleague – The individuals do not need explanation as they can be representative, except that this would be a place just to plant a small marker to the most flamboyant man I ever met, the Baron Paul de Gaiffier d'Hestroy (two particules, no less), who died young many years ago. On being asked advice on buying a suit and being told (in the late 1970s) that the budget was £80, he declared: "But my dear you can't buy a sleeve for that!" He then added, "But these tailors are all crooks, you know," as if anyone else on the school staff had a tailor. He was enormous fun. *Salut.*

The What Ifs – The sugary confection Brighton rock was famed for the 'writing going all the way through' (e.g. in Graham Greene's novel *Brighton Rock*, the character Ida says, 'It's like those sticks of rock: bite it all the way down, you'll still read Brighton'). Verse 7 refers to John Donne's poem *A Nocturnal upon Saint Lucy's Day* which is thought to have been written in 1627, the year in which both his great friend, Lucy Countess of Bedford, and his young daughter Lucy died. He writes: 'I am re-begot/ Of absence, darkness, death – things which are not.' Verse 8 references Greek mythology: Prometheus' punishment for giving fire back to mankind was to be chained to a rock and have his liver eaten by an eagle each day, while the liver regenerated each night. Sisyphus was a king punished by being compelled to roll an immense boulder up a hill, only to watch it roll back down just as he got near the top, and to repeat this throughout eternity.

Scafell Pike – is the highest mountain in England, situated in the Lake District. Line 6: no disrespect to Wilfrid Owen's poem *Dulce et Decorum Est*, but a reusing of his phrase 'old beggars under sacks' as the description is physically apt. Line 8: 'rime' is a word used more in mountaineering than life in general and means frosted covering. Line13: an echo from *Macbeth* to bring to mind the 'vaulting ambition' referred to in the play's next line. Line 14: a reversal of the mountaineer George Mallory's famous dictum of climbing 'because it's there', but I think a truer motivation.

WW1 War Grave, Equancourt – This visitors' book entry is actually dated 1985, which seemed quite shocking when I read it in the early 1990s. Yet if born in the last year of World War One, the writer need only then have been 67 years old. The events of 1914-1918 still echo down the years. As time has passed I have taken the liberty of adding ten years to the entry date to keep it closer to the present, while keeping it still feasible, but I cannot do so again.

Night Exercise – This began with the thought that a soldier with a spade can be more frightening than a soldier with a gun and also my wondering (without conclusion) whether at gunpoint I would consent to dig my own grave for the sake of the few extra minutes of life that might afford.

Lunacy – There are references to *Swan Lake* and the legend of Brigadoon (based on an older German story about the mythical village of Germelshausen), a village that appears only once every hundred years. The idea of faith (not imagination) being strong enough to move mountains can be found in the Bible (Matthew ch 21 v. 21, Mark ch. 11, v. 23).

The Long View – Giulio Libri, Professor of Aristotelian Philosophy at Pisa, famously refused to look through Galileo's telescope when invited to do so and see for himself the phenomenon that Galileo argued supported the then disputed heliocentric theory of Copernicus. It may seem odd to our scientific age, but Libri had three good reasons: it was well known that a single lens could distort and so the combination of two lenses could be regarded as introducing more aberrations; trusting one's eyes alone was dangerous as it was (and is) well known that we frequently see things differently to each other and are often mistaken in what we think we have seen; a geocentric universe placed earth and man at the centre of God's creation, whereas a heliocentric universe did not, and so heliocentricity had profound religious and philosophical implications affecting the ingrained knowledge, beliefs and traditions by which Libri and others lived their lives. The rhythm for this poem is partly borrowed from Kipling's *Gunga Din*, as is the phrase 'by the living God that made me' so introducing a certain irony by subterfuge, as Kipling's poem ends:

> By the livin Gawd that made you.
> You're a better man than I am, Gunga Din!

For performance in family/junior locations I use an alternative ending that is less blunt in its language:

> To turn God's plan to farce
> for what appears through bits of glass
> is a folly we can all well do without.

It is weaker, but not fatal to the idea.

Technical Rehearsal – As part of the technical rehearsals in a theatre an actor or other person may be required to stand in certain marked places while the lighting effects are checked on faces and costumes, for any unwanted shadows and so forth. Line 6: at the end of *A Midsummer Night's Dream*, Puck refers to actors as shadows ('If we shadows have offended...'). Line 8: light was created on the first day according to the Book of Genesis. Any connection between 'fuse' and The Big Bang is more verbal than scientific, as I am woefully ignorant of the origin of light in Big Bang theory. Line 14: a can is type of stage light and shutters are used to modify the light cast.

Since there's no help – Michael Drayton is not best known as a sonneteer, but the influence of this sonnet on my work should be pretty clear. The move from a robust declaration of independence to an ingratiating wheedle is wonderfully childlike as well as fitting the dependent lover. It is here in this book both because I feel it should be better known and because there was a time, as Dana Gioia remarked in his essay *Can Poetry Matter?* (http://www.danagioia.net/essays/ecpm.htm), when poets would include other poets' works in their recitals. A single poem by another author in this volume may be a very small sharing, but it is something. I do recommend Gioia's essay much of which seems to me to be as pertinent now as when written in 1991 – as with this extract:

> *Why, for example, does poetry mix so seldom with music, dance, or theater? At most readings the program consists of verse only – and usually only verse by that night's author. Forty years ago, when Dylan Thomas read, he spent half the program reciting other poets' work. Hardly a self-effacing man, he was nevertheless humble before his art. Today most readings are celebrations less of poetry than of the author's ego. No wonder the audience for such events usually consists entirely of poets, would-be poets, and friends of the author.*

The Voice of God – When I was very young and heard, usually at Christmas, the Bible passage about the fall of Adam and Eve, when 'they heard the voice of the Lord God walking in the garden' and hid because they knew they were naked, I always imagined that it was the *voice* that was somehow walking, rather than that they heard the voice of *God* who was walking. Well, God was different so why should his voice not be embodied on its own? I've never quite lost that childhood interpretation. 3rd stanza: the lost Adamic language is typically identified with either the language used by God to address Adam in Eden, or the language invented by Adam, in either case supposedly bearing a much stronger relationship between the word and the thing than mere representation. Last stanza: '*omnia unum est*' means 'all things are one'.

Bar Talk – Line 12: I am against using poetic abbreviations (e.g. ne'er for never) but when I act this, I use something of a (not too strong) East End London accent because it seems to work. Dropping aitches leads me in line 12 to say, 'there's no-one 'ome, 'cept pain...' Contracting 'except' sounds just right in this instance, even though it does not look very good in print.

Osric's Tale – *Hamlet V ii:* Osric is the flamboyant and rather fey professional courtier who on behalf of King Claudius delivers the challenge to Hamlet for the fencing match with Laertes, which as a result of treachery, involving a poisoned sword and a poisoned drink, will leave the dead bodies of Hamlet, Laertes, Claudius and Queen Gertrude on the stage at the end of the play. When delivering the challenge, Osric is mocked by Hamlet and his friend Horatio for excessive use of ultra-fashionable words and for flourishing his hat when he speaks. Early on in the encounter, Hamlet turns to Horatio and asks, 'Dost know this waterfly?' At the end of the play, the professional courtier Osric must be in a difficult position. With the immediate Danish royal house all lying dead on the stage and the young Norwegian hothead Fortinbras arriving at that point with, as it happens, a substantial army at his back, the old certainties of court life are surely swept away in favour of new rules that are not yet clear.

En Passant – Samuel Taylor Coleridge claimed to have perceived the entire course of the poem *Kubla Khan* in a dream (possibly opium-induced), but was interrupted by a visitor from Porlock while in the process of writing it. After that meeting he could recall very little and the poem is therefore only 54 lines long and incomplete.